I0435074

United States
Department of
Agriculture

Forest Service

**Northern
Research Station**

Resource Bulletin
NRS-70

Assessing Urban Forest Effects and Values: Morgantown's Urban Forest

David J. Nowak
Robert E. Hoehn III
Daniel E. Crane
Jack C. Stevens
Jonathan Cumming
Sandhya Mohen
Anne Buckelew Cumming

Abstract

An analysis of the community forest in Morgantown, WV, was undertaken in 2004 to characterize the structural and functional attributes of this forest resource. The assessment revealed that this city has about 658,000 trees with canopies that cover 35.5 percent of the area. The most common tree species are sugar maple, black cherry, and hawthorn. The urban forest currently stores about 93,000 tons of carbon valued at $1.9 million. In addition, these trees remove about 2,900 tons of carbon per year ($60,000 per year), with trees and shrubs removing about 104 tons of air pollution per year ($711,000 per year). Trees in Morgantown are estimated to reduce annual residential energy costs by $380,000 per year. The structural, or compensatory, value is estimated at $488 million. Information on the structure and functions of the urban forest can be used to improve and augment support for urban forest management programs and to integrate urban forests within plans to improve environmental quality in the Morgantown, WV area.

Cover Photo

View of Morgantown, WV, from the Monongahela River. Photo by Anne Cumming, U.S. Forest Service.

Assessing Urban Forest Effects and Values: Morgantown's Urban Forest

David J. Nowak
Robert E. Hoehn III
Daniel E. Crane
Jack C. Stevens
Jonathan Cumming
Sandhya Mohen
Anne Buckelew Cumming

The Authors

DAVID J. NOWAK is a research forester and project leader with the U.S. Forest Service's Northern Research Station at Syracuse, New York.

ROBERT E. HOEHN III is a forester with the U.S. Forest Service's Northern Research Station at Syracuse, New York.

DANIEL E. CRANE is an information technology specialist with the U.S. Forest Service's Northern Research Station at Syracuse, New York.

JACK C. STEVENS is a retired forester with the U.S. Forest Service's Northern Research Station at Syracuse, NY.

JONATHAN CUMMING is a professor in the Department of Biology at West Virginia University.

SANDHYA MOHEN was a graduate student at West Virginia University.

ANNE BUCKELEW CUMMING is a forester with the US Forest Service's State and Private Forestry in Morgantown, West Virginia.

Photo by Anne Cumming, U.S. Forest Service

EXECUTIVE SUMMARY

Trees in cities can contribute significantly to human health and environmental quality. Unfortunately, little is known about the urban forest resource and what it contributes to the local and regional society and economy. To better understand the urban forest resource and its numerous values, the USDA Forest Service, Northern Research Station, developed the i-Tree Eco model (formerly Urban Forest Effects [UFORE] model). Results from this model are used to advance the understanding of the urban forest resource, improve urban forest policies, planning and management, provide data for the potential inclusion of trees within environmental regulations, and determine how trees affect the environment and consequently enhance human health and environmental quality in urban areas.

Forest structure is a measure of various physical attributes of the vegetation, such as tree species composition, number of trees, tree density, tree health, leaf area, biomass, and species diversity. Forest functions, which are determined by forest structure, include a wide range of environmental and ecosystem services, such as air pollution removal and cooler air temperatures. Forest values are an estimate of the economic worth of the various forest functions.

To help determine the vegetation structure, functions, and values of the urban forest in Morgantown, WV, a vegetation assessment was conducted during the summer of 2004. For this assessment, one-tenth acre field plots were sampled and analyzed using the i-Tree Eco model. This report summarizes results and values of:

- Forest structure
- Potential risk to forest from insects or diseases
- Air pollution removal
- Carbon storage
- Annual carbon removal (sequestration)
- Changes in building energy use

> Urban forests provide numerous benefits to society, yet relatively little is known about this important resource in Morgantown.
>
> In 2004, the i-Tree Eco (formerly UFORE) model was used to survey and analyze Morgantown's urban forest.
>
> The calculated environmental benefits of the urban forest are significant, yet many environmental and social benefits still remain to be quantified.

i-Tree

Table 1.—Summary statistics for Morgantown's urban forest

Feature	Estimate
Number of trees	658,000
Tree cover	35.5%
Most common species	sugar maple, black cherry, hawthorn
Trees < 6 inches diameter	70.2%
Pollution removal	104 tons/year ($711,000/year)
Carbon storage	93,000 tons ($1.9 million)
Carbon sequestration	2,900 tons/year ($60,000/year)
Building energy reduction	$380,000 / year
Avoided carbon emissions	$18,500 / year
Structural value	$488 million

Ton – short ton (U.S.) (2,000 lbs)

I-TREE ECO MODEL AND FIELD MEASUREMENTS

Urban forests have many functions and values. To help characterize the values for Morgantown's urban forest, data from 136 field plots located throughout the city were analyzed using the i-Tree Eco model.[1]

i-Tree Eco uses standardized field data from randomly located plots and local hourly air pollution and meteorological data to quantify urban forest structure and its numerous effects, including:

- Urban forest structure (e.g., species composition, tree density, tree health, leaf area, leaf and tree biomass, species diversity, etc.).
- Amount of pollution removed hourly by the urban forest and its associated percent air quality improvement throughout a year. Pollution removal is calculated for ozone, sulfur dioxide, nitrogen dioxide, carbon monoxide, and particulate matter (<10 microns).
- Total carbon stored and net carbon annually sequestered by the urban forest.
- Effects of trees on building energy use and consequent effects on carbon dioxide emissions from power plants.
- Compensatory value of the forest, as well as the value of air pollution removal and carbon storage and sequestration.
- Potential impact of infestations by Asian longhorned beetles, emerald ash borers, gypsy moth, or Dutch elm disease.

In the field, one-tenth acre plots were randomly located within different land-use strata of Morgantown. These land uses were used to divide the analysis into smaller zones. The plots were divided among the following land uses: cemeteries & vacant (8 plots), commercial & services (17 plots), farm (10 plots), forest (18 plots), high-density residential (40 plots), institutional (17 plots), low-density residential (4 plots), park (6 plots), transportation rights-of-way (11 plots), and urban forest corridor (5 plots). Land-use strata were established by visually delineating land use using digital images of Morgantown, WV (Table 2).

Field data were collected by West Virginia University personnel. Data collection occurred during the leaf-on season to properly assess tree canopies. Within each plot, data included land use, ground and tree cover, shrub characteristics, and individual tree attributes of species, including stem diameter at breast height (d.b.h.; measured at 4.5 ft.), tree height, height to base of live crown, crown width, percentage crown canopy missing and dieback, and distance and direction to residential buildings.[2]

To estimate current carbon storage, biomass for each tree was calculated using equations from the literature and measured tree data. Open-grown, maintained trees tend to have less biomass than predicted by forest-derived biomass equations.[3] To adjust for this difference, biomass results for open-grown urban trees are multiplied by 0.8.[3] No adjustment is made for trees found in natural stand conditions. Tree dry-weight biomass was converted to stored carbon by multiplying by 0.5.

Table 2.—Land-use designations

Land Use	Description
Cemeteries & vacant	Cemeteries and land that was devoid of structures and excluded from the other land use classes
Commercial & services	Urban business districts, shopping centers, commercial strip developments
Farm	Row crops, pasture, horticulture areas, orchards; Used for production of food and fiber
Forest	Woodlots that are at least 1.0 acre in size, 120 feet wide for at least 363 feet
High-density residential	Residential areas where houses were on lots less than 1.0 acre, typically with linear driveways, lawns and structures with uniform size and spacing
Institutional	Educational and health facilities, including buildings, grounds and parking lots so designated for this land use
Low-density residential	Residential areas where houses were on lots greater than 1.0 acre
Park	Urban recreational parks, golf driving ranges, sports fields
Transportation rights-of-way	Highways, and highway facilities including rights of way and area used for interchanges; railways and rail facilities such as tracks, spur connections, stations; airports, runways, intervening land and buffer zone
Urban forest corridor	Woodlots less than 1.0 acre in size and less than 120 feet wide and 363 feet long

To estimate the gross amount of carbon sequestered annually, average diameter growth from the appropriate genera and diameter class and tree condition was added to the existing tree diameter (year x) to estimate tree diameter and carbon storage in year $x+1$.

Air pollution removal estimates are derived from calculated hourly tree-canopy resistances for ozone, and sulfur and nitrogen dioxides based on a hybrid of big-leaf and multi-layer canopy deposition models.[4, 5] As the removal of carbon monoxide and particulate matter by vegetation is not directly related to transpiration, removal rates (deposition velocities) for these pollutants were based on average measured values from the literature[6, 7] that were adjusted depending on leaf phenology and leaf area. Particulate removal incorporated a 50 percent resuspension rate of particles back to the atmosphere.[8]

Seasonal effects of trees on residential building energy use was calculated based on procedures described in the literature[9] using distance and direction of trees from residential structures, tree height, and tree condition data.

Compensatory values were based on valuation procedures of the Council of Tree and Landscape Appraisers[10], which uses tree species, diameter, condition, and location information.[10]

Additional details about i-Tree Eco methods[11] are available at: http://www.nrs.fs.fed.us/tools/UFORE/ and http://www.itreetools.org.

TREE CHARACTERISTICS OF THE URBAN FOREST

The urban forest of Morgantown (2004) has an estimated 658,000 trees with a tree cover of 35.5 percent. Trees in this study are defined as woody plants with a d.b.h. of at least 1 inch. The three most common species in the urban forest are sugar maple (14.9 percent), black cherry (7.9 percent), and hawthorn (4.8 percent). The 10 most common species account for 54.9 percent of all trees (Fig. 1).

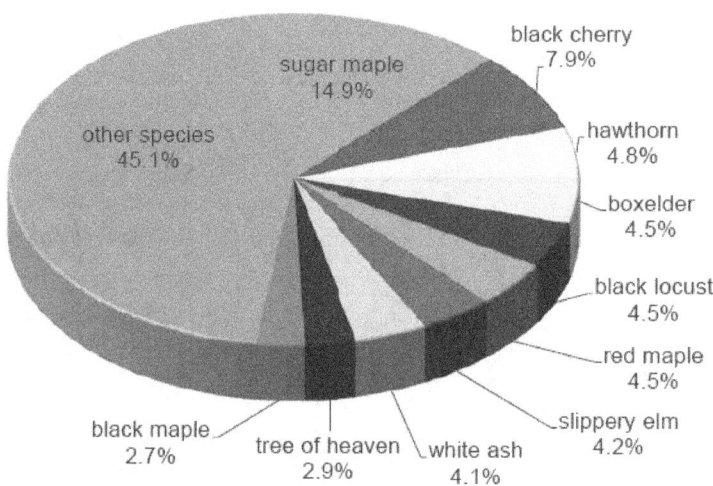

Figure 1.—Species composition of 10 most common species in Morgantown, WV, 2004.

The highest density of trees occurs in the urban forest corridors (530 trees/acre), followed by forest land (316 trees/acre), and the low-density residential areas (160 trees/acre) (Fig. 2). The greatest number of trees is in the forest (278,800), followed by high density residential (147,900), and urban forest corridors (141,500) (Fig. 2). This abundance distribution is a reflection of the dominance of trees in the forest, high-density residential, and urban forest corridor land-use types. The tree density in Morgantown is 119.2 trees/acre, which is the highest value among cities with tree density data, with a range from 9.1 to 119.2 trees/acre (Appendix I). This high density is partially due to topographic constraint to urban development in West Virginia. Morgantown is in the Appalachian Plateau Province, which is bisected by numerous valleys. The average slope of the sampled i-Tree Eco plots was 14.4 percent.

There are an estimated 658,000 trees in Morgantown with canopies that cover 35.5% of the city.

Tree density is highest in the urban forest corridors and lowest in the farm land.

Nearly 77% of the tree species in Morgantown are native to West Virginia.

i-Tree

Trees that have diameters less than 6 inches account for 70.2 percent of the population (Fig. 3). The size distribution of trees in Morgantown follows a reverse J-shaped curve, which is typical of native mixed-aged forests and urban and community forests. This pattern most likely reflects differential growth rates of the various species within the urban forest as well as continual tree replacement through mortality and invasion in nonmanaged land uses and landscape replacement, planting, and removals in intensively managed land uses.

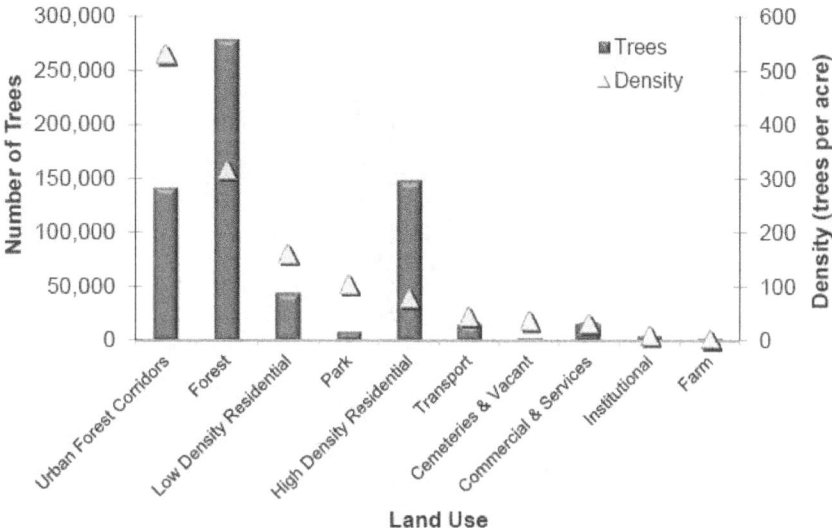

Figure 2.—Number of trees and tree density by land use, Morgantown, WV, 2004.

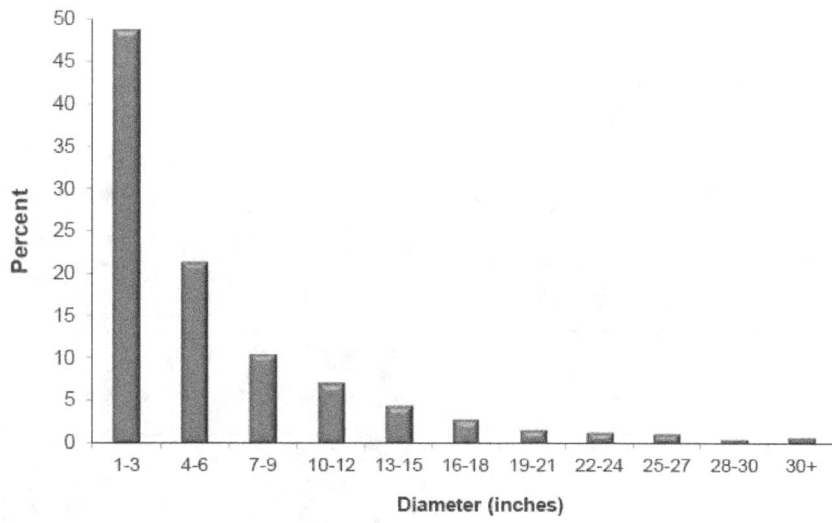

Figure 3.—Percent of tree population by diameter (d.b.h.) class, Morgantown, WV, 2004.

Urban forests are a mix of native tree species that existed prior to development and exotic species that were introduced by residents or other means. Thus, urban forests often have a tree diversity that is higher than surrounding native landscapes. Increased tree diversity can minimize the overall impact or destruction by a species-specific insect or disease, but the increase in the number of exotic plants can also pose a risk to native plants if some of the exotics species are invasive plants that can potentially out-compete and displace native species. In Morgantown, about 77 percent of the trees are species native to West Virginia (Fig. 4). Trees with a native origin outside of North America are mostly from Asia (3.9 percent of the species).

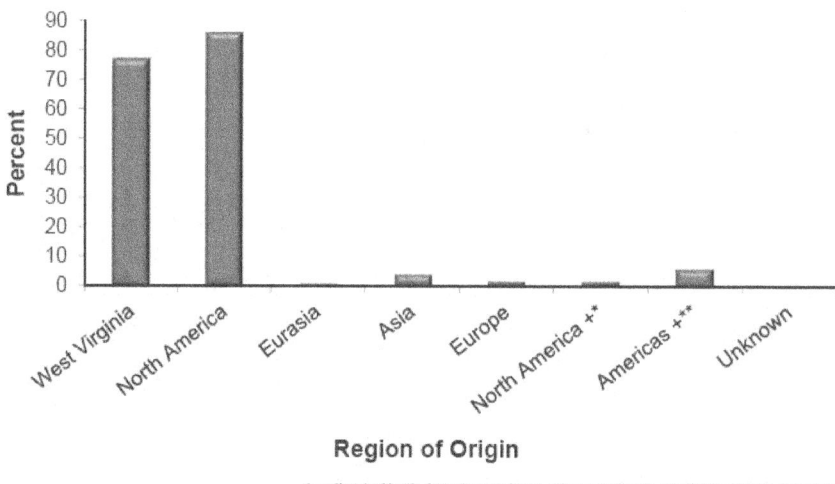

* native to North America and one other continent, excluding South America
** native to North America and South America, and one other continent

Figure 4.—Percent of tree population by area of origin, Morgantown, WV, 2004.

Urban forests are a mix of native tree species that existed prior to development and exotic species that were introduced by residents or other means.

i-Tree

URBAN FOREST COVER AND LEAF AREA

Urban forests and landscapes present a wide variety of cover types that influence the function of the urban forest. Certain cover types, for example trees and shrubs, help mitigate stormwater pulses, whereas impervious surfaces exacerbate runoff and may increase ambient temperatures. At the time of the 2004 sampling, trees covered about 35.5 percent of Morgantown and shrubs cover 21.2 percent of the city. Dominant ground-cover types include herbaceous (51.8 percent), impervious surfaces (excluding buildings) (20.0 percent), and duff/mulch cover (13.7 percent) (Fig. 5).

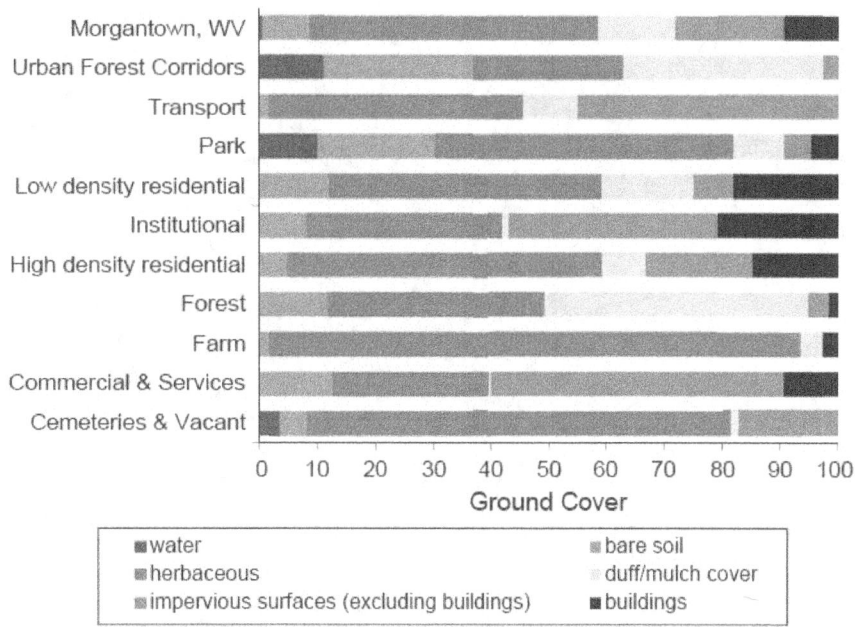

Figure 5.—Percent of land-use area covered by ground cover classes, Morgantown, WV, 2004.

Photo by Jonathan Cumming, West Virginia University, used with permission

Many urban forest benefits, such as temperature moderation, carbon capture, and pollutant removal, are linked directly to the amount of healthy leaf surface area of the trees. In Morgantown, trees that dominate in terms of leaf area are sugar maple, black cherry, and red maple (Fig. 6).

Tree species with relatively large individuals contributing leaf area to the population (species with percent of leaf area much greater than percent of total population) are American sycamore, northern red oak, and tulip tree. Smaller trees in the population are hawthorn, black haw, and sassafras.

A species contribution to the urban forest can be described with an "importance value" (IV), which is calculated form a formula using species' relative leaf area and abundance (Fig. 6). The most important species in Morgantown's urban forest, according to IVs, are sugar maple, black cherry, and red maple (Table 3).

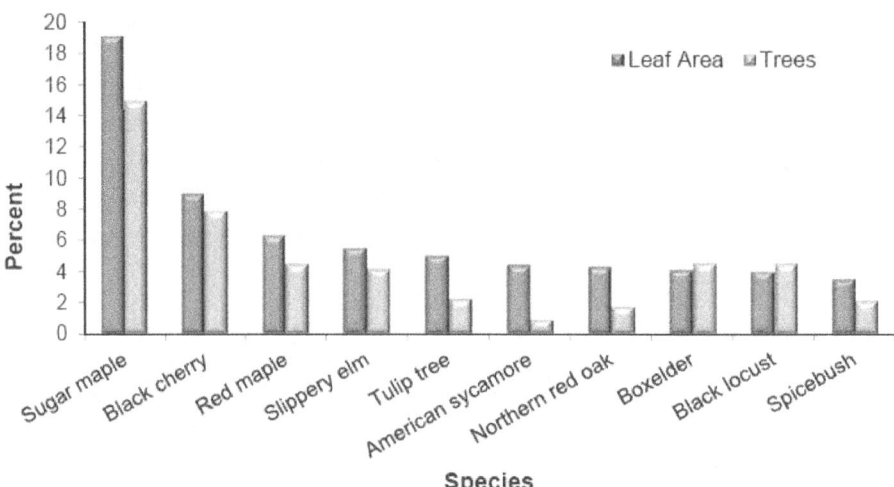

Figure 6.—Percent of total tree population and total leaf area for the 10 most common tree species, Morgantown, WV, 2004.

Table 3.—Percent of total population, percent of total leaf and importance values of species with the greatest importance values

Common Name	%Pop[a]	%LA[b]	IV[c]
Sugar maple	14.9	19.1	34.0
Black cherry	7.9	9.0	16.9
Red maple	4.5	6.3	10.8
Slippery elm	4.2	5.5	9.7
Boxelder	4.5	4.1	8.6
Black locust	4.5	4.0	8.5
Tulip tree	2.2	5.0	7.2
Northern red oak	1.7	4.3	6.0
White ash	4.1	1.9	6.0
Black maple	2.7	3.2	5.9

[a] percent of population
[b] percent of leaf area
[c] %Pop + %LA

Healthy leaf area equates directly to tree benefits provided to the community.

Sugar maple has the greatest importance in Morgantown's urban forest based on relative leaf area and relative population.

i-Tree

AIR POLLUTION REMOVAL BY URBAN TREES

Poor air quality is a common problem in many urban areas. It can lead to human health problems, damage to landscape materials and ecosystem processes, and reduced visibility. The urban forest can help improve air quality by reducing air temperature, directly removing pollutants from the air, and reducing energy consumption in buildings, which consequently reduce air pollutant emissions from power plants. Trees also emit volatile organic compounds that can contribute to ozone formation. However, integrative studies have revealed that an increase in tree cover leads to reduced ozone formation.[12]

Pollution removal by trees and shrubs in Morgantown was estimated using the i-Tree Eco model in conjunction with field data and hourly pollution and weather data for the year 2000. Pollution removal was greatest for ozone (O_3), followed by particulate matter less than ten microns (PM_{10}), sulfur dioxide (SO_2), nitrogen dioxide (NO_2), and carbon monoxide (CO) (Fig. 7). It is estimated that trees and shrubs remove 104 tons of air pollution (CO, NO_2, O_3, PM_{10}, SO_2) per year with an associated value of $711,000 (based on estimated 2007 national median externality costs associated with pollutants[13]). Trees remove about 2.2 times more air pollution than shrubs in Morgantown.

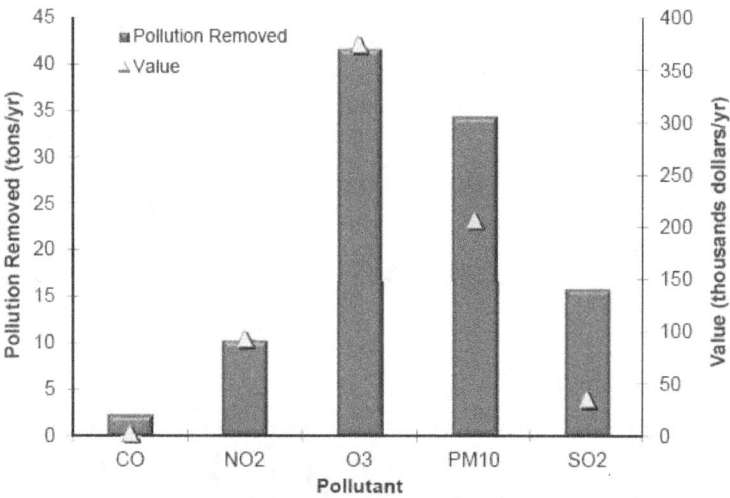

Figure 7.—Annual air pollution removal and value by trees and shrubs in Morgantown, WV, 2000

Table 4.—Estimated percent air quality improvement by trees during the in-leaf season, Morgantown, WV, 2000		
Pollutant	Average Effects[a]	Peak Effects
PM_{10}	1.1%	14.8%
O_3	0.7%	10.4%
SO_2	0.7%	10.0%
NO_2	0.5%	6.8%
CO	0.003%	0.05%

[a] daytime

The average hourly percentage of air quality improvement removed by trees during the daytime, in-leaf season was typically less than 1 percent, but peak effects were up to around 15 percent in heavily-treed areas (Table 4).

General recommendations for air quality improvement with trees are given in Appendix II.

CARBON STORAGE AND SEQUESTRATION

Climate change is an issue of global concern to many people. Carbon storage by trees is one way that trees influence global climate change. Urban trees can help mitigate climate change by sequestering atmospheric carbon (from carbon dioxide) in tissues and by reducing energy use in buildings, consequently reducing carbon dioxide emissions from fossil fuel based power plants.[14]

Trees reduce the amount of carbon in the atmosphere by sequestering carbon in new tissue growth every year. As trees grow, they store more carbon by holding it in their accumulated tissues (roots, stems, branches, and leaves). The amount of carbon annually sequestered is increased with healthier trees and larger diameter trees. As trees die and decay, they release much of the stored carbon back to the atmosphere. Thus, carbon storage is the amount of carbon that can be lost if trees are allowed to die and decompose.

At the time of sampling, trees in Morgantown stored 93,000 tons of carbon, and much of this was stored in intermediate-size trees and in trees greater than 30 inch d.b.h. (Fig. 8). This pattern reflects the importance of accumulated wood in storing fixed carbon. In contrast, the rate of carbon sequestration was highest in the smaller diameter tree classes (Fig. 8), reflecting differences in growth rates, tree condition, and number of trees among diameter classes. The accumulated stored carbon in Morgantown's urban forest has an estimated ecosystem service value of $1.9 million.

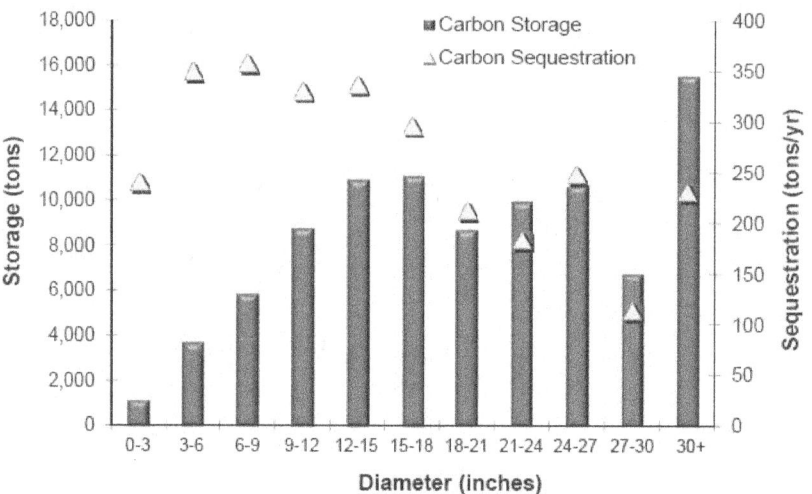

Figure 8.—Estimated carbon storage and sequestration by diameter class, Morgantown, WV, 2004.

i-Tree

Urban forests may play important roles in capturing and storing carbon dioxide from the atmosphere. Net carbon sequestration is positive in healthy and actively growing trees, but can be negative if emission of carbon from decomposition is greater than sequestration by healthy trees.

Gross carbon sequestration by trees in Morgantown was about 2,900 tons of carbon per year with an associated value of $60,000 annually (Fig. 9). Net carbon sequestration, which is gross sequestration adjusted for estimated carbon losses due to tree mortality (e.g., from decomposition, burning) was estimated at 2,300 tons. Of all the species sampled, black cherry stored and sequestered the most carbon (17.4 percent of all sequestered carbon and 20.7 percent of the total carbon stored). Sugar maple was the next most important species in carbon capture (15.7 percent of all carbon sequestered and 10.9 percent of the total carbon stored) (Fig. 9).

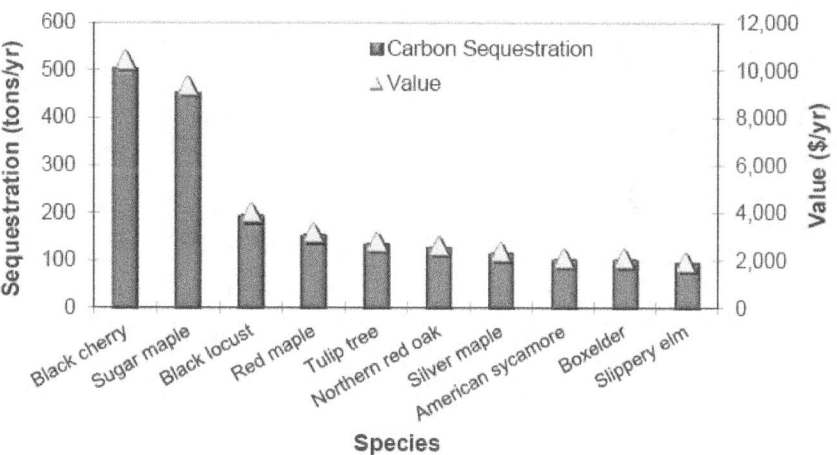

Figure 9.—Estimated annual carbon sequestration and value for the tree species with the greatest total sequestration, Morgantown, WV, 2004.

Photo by Anne Cumming, U.S. Forest Service

Carbon storage:
Carbon currently held in tree tissue (roots, stems, and branches) in Morgantown's urban forest is 93,000 tons valued at $1.9 million.

Carbon sequestration:
The estimated amount of carbon removed annually by Morgantown's trees is 2,900 tons/year with a value of $60,000 annually.

i-Tree

TREES AFFECT ENERGY USE IN BUILDINGS

Trees affect energy consumption by shading buildings, providing evaporative cooling, and blocking winter winds. Trees tend to reduce building energy consumption in the summer months and can either increase or decrease building energy use in the winter months, depending on the location of trees around the building. Estimates of tree effects on energy use are based on field measurements of tree distance and direction to space-conditioned residential buildings.[9]

Based on average energy costs in West Virginia in 2007, trees in Morgantown are estimated to reduce energy use (Table 5) and costs (Table 6) from residential buildings by $380,000 annually. Trees also provide an additional $18,500 in value per year by reducing the amount of carbon released by fossil-fuel based power plants (a reduction of 900 tons of carbon emissions).

Table 5.—Annual energy savings due to trees near residential buildings

	Heating	Cooling	Total
MBTU[a]	15,100	n/a	15,100
MWH[b]	200	2,200	2,400
Carbon avoided (t)	300	600	900

[a]Million British Thermal Units
[b]Megawatt-hour

Table 6.—Annual savings[c] (U.S. $) in residential energy expenditures during heating and cooling seasons

	Heating	Cooling	Total
MBTU[a]	$219,000	n/a	$219,000
MWH[b]	$16,000	$145,000	$161,000
Carbon avoided	$6,100	$12,400	$18,500

[a]Million British Thermal Units
[b]Megawatt-hour
[c]Based on state-wide energy costs

> **Trees affect energy consumption by shading buildings, providing evaporative cooling, and blocking winter winds.**
>
> **Interactions between buildings and trees save an estimated $380,000 per year in heating and cooling costs.**
>
> **Lower energy use in residential buildings reduced carbon emissions from power plants by 900 tons per year ($18,500 per year).**

i-Tree

STRUCTURAL AND FUNCTIONAL VALUES

Urban forests have a structural value based on the tree itself, including compensatory value and carbon storage value. The structural value[10] of an urban forest tends to increase with an increase in the number and size of healthy trees. The structural value of the urban forest in Morgantown is about $488 million (Fig. 10).

Urban forests also have functional values (either positive or negative) based on the functions the tree performs (e.g., carbon sequestration and pollution removal). Annual functional values also tend to increase with increased number and size of healthy trees, and are usually on the order of several million dollars per year. There are many other functional values of the urban forest, although they are not quantified here (e.g., reduction in air temperatures and ultraviolet radiation, improvements in water quality). Thus, these functional values are conservative estimates of the actual contributions of the urban forest. Through proper and management, urban forest values can be increased. In contrast, the values and benefits also can decrease as the amount of healthy tree cover declines.

Structural values:
- Compensatory value: $488 million
- Carbon storage: $1.9 million

Annual functional values:
- Carbon sequestration: $60,000
- Pollution removal: $711,000
- Lower energy costs and reduced carbon emissions: $398,500

More detailed information on the urban forest in Morgantown (e.g., species breakdowns by land use) can be found at http://www.nrs.fs.fed.us/data/urban. Additionally, information comparing tree benefits to estimates of average carbons emissions in the city, average automobile emissions, and average household emissions can be found in Appendix III; a priority planting index map can be found in Appendix IV, and a list of species sampled can be found in Appendix V.

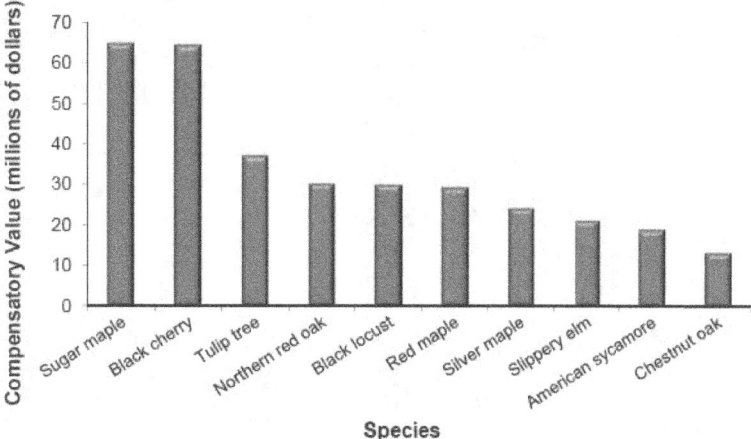

Figure 10.—Structural or compensatory value of the tree species with the greatest structural value, Morgantown, WV, 2004.

POTENTIAL INSECT AND DISEASE IMPACTS

Various insects and diseases can infest urban forests, potentially killing trees and reducing the health, value, and sustainability of the urban forest. As pests have different tree hosts, the potential damage or risk of each pest will differ. Four exotic pests were analyzed for their potential impact: Asian longhorned beetle, gypsy moth, emerald ash borer, and Dutch elm disease (Fig. 11).

Asian longhorned beetle

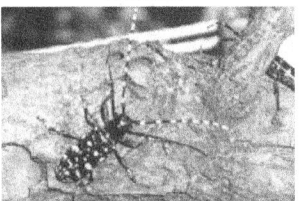

Kenneth R. Law
USDA APHIS PPQ
(www.invasive.org)

The Asian longhorned beetle (ALB)[15] is an insect that bores into and kills a wide range of hardwood species. This beetle was discovered in 1996 in Brooklyn, NY, and has subsequently spread to Long Island, Queens, and Manhattan. In 1998, the beetle was discovered in the suburbs of Chicago, IL. Beetles have also been found in Jersey City, NJ (2002), Toronto/Vaughan, Ontario (2003), and Middlesex/Union Counties, NJ (2004). In 2007, the beetle was found on Staten and Prall's Island, NY. Most recently, beetles were detected in Worcester, MA (2008). ALB represents a potential loss to the Morgantown urban forest of $298 million in compensatory value (54.3 percent of the population).

The gypsy moth (GM)[16] is a defoliator that feeds on many species causing widespread defoliation and tree death if outbreak conditions last several years. This pest could potentially result in damage to or a loss of $57 million in compensatory value (8.6 percent of the population).

Emerald ash borer

David Cappaert
Michigan State University
(www.invasive.org)

Since being discovered in Detroit in 2002, emerald ash borer (EAB)[17] has killed millions of ash trees in several states in the East and Midwest. EAB has the potential to affect 6.0 percent of the population ($12 million in compensatory value).

American elm, one of the most important street trees in the 20th century, has been devastated by the Dutch elm disease (DED). Since first reported in the 1930s, DED has killed more than 50 percent of the native elm population in the United States.[18] Although some elm species have shown varying degrees of resistance, Morgantown could lose up to 5.7 percent of its trees to this disease ($25 million in compensatory value).

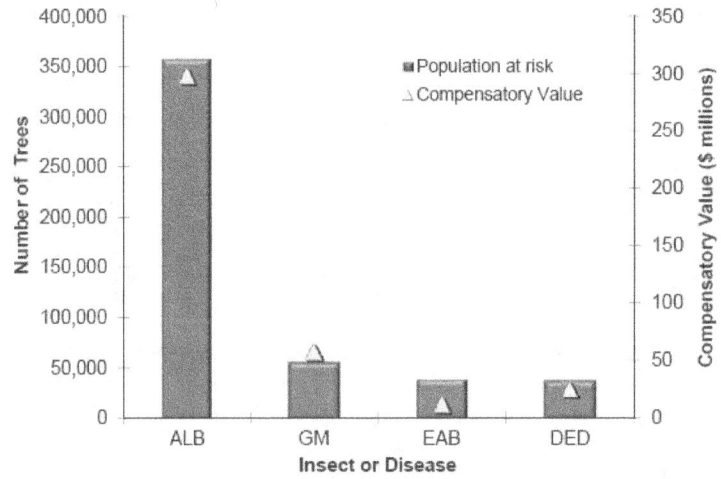

Figure 11.—Number of trees and value potentially affected by various insects and diseases, Morgantown, WV, 2004.

APPENDIX I.—COMPARISON OF URBAN FORESTS

A commonly asked question is, "How does this city compare to other cities?" Although comparison among cities should be made with caution as there are many attributes of a city that affect urban forest structure and functions, summary data are provided from other cities analyzed using the i-Tree Eco (UFORE) model.

I. City totals, trees only

City	% Tree cover[a]	Number of trees	Carbon storage (tons)	Carbon sequestration (tons/yr)	Pollution removal (tons/yr)[b]	Pollution value U.S. $[c]
Calgary, Alberta[d*]	7.2	11,889,000	445,000	21,400	326	2,357,000
Toronto, Ontario[d]	26.6	10,220,000	1,221,000	51,500	2,099	17,146,000
Atlanta, GA[e]	53.9	9,415,000	1,344,000	46,400	1,663	12,213,000
Los Angeles, CA[f]	20.6	5,993,000	1,269,000	77,000	1,976	14,173,000
New York, NY[e]	20.9	5,212,000	1,350,000	42,300	1,677	11,834,000
Chicago, IL[g]	18.0	3,585,000	716,000	25,200	888	6,398,000
Baltimore, MD[h]	28.5	2,479,000	570,000	18,400	430	3,123,000
Philadelphia, PA[e]	20.8	2,113,000	530,000	16,100	576	4,150,000
Washington, DC[i]	35.0	1,928,000	526,000	16,200	418	2,858,000
Oakville, Ontario[j]	29.1	1,908,000	147,000	6,600	190	1,421,000
Scranton, PA[k]	22.0	1,198,000	93,000	4,000	72	514,000
Boston, MA[e]	28.9	1,183,000	319,000	10,500	284	2,092,000
Syracuse, NY[h]	26.9	1,088,000	183,000	5,900	109	836,000
Woodbridge, NJ[l*]	29.5	986,000	160,000	5,600	210	1,525,000
Minneapolis, MN[m]	34.1	979,000	250,000	8,900	306	2,242,000
San Francisco, CA[d]	16.0	668,000	194,000	5,100	141	1,018,000
Morgantown, WV[n*]	35.5	658,000	93,000	2,900	104	711,000
Moorestown, NJ[l*]	28.0	583,000	117,000	3,800	118	841,000
Jersey City, NJ[l*]	11.5	136,000	21,000	890	41	292,000
Casper, WY[d*]	8.9	123,000	37,000	1,200	37	275,000
Freehold, NJ[l]	31.2	48,000	20,000	550	22	162,000

II. Per acre values of tree effects

City	No. of trees	Carbon Storage (tons)	Carbon sequestration (tons/yr)	Pollution removal (lbs/yr)	Pollution value U.S. $[1]
Calgary, Alberta[d]	66.7	2.5	0.12	3.7	13.2
Toronto, Ontario[d]	64.9	7.8	0.33	26.7	108.9
Atlanta, GA[e]	111.6	15.9	0.55	39.4	144.8
Los Angeles, CA[f]	19.9	4.2	0.26	13.1	47.1
New York, NY[e]	26.4	6.8	0.21	17.0	59.9
Chicago, IL[g]	24.3	4.8	0.17	12.0	43.3
Baltimore, MD[h]	48.0	11.0	0.36	16.6	60.4
Philadelphia, PA[e]	25.1	6.3	0.19	13.6	49.2
Washington, DC[i]	49.0	13.4	0.41	21.2	72.7
Oakville, Ontario[j]	55.6	4.3	0.19	11.0	41.4

Continued

APPENDIX I.—CONTINUED

City	No. of trees	Carbon Storage (tons)	Carbon sequestration (tons/yr)	Pollution removal (lbs/yr)	Pollution value U.S. $[1]
Scranton, PA[k]	116.4	9.1	0.39	13.9	49.9
Boston, MA[e]	33.5	9.1	0.30	16.1	59.3
Syracuse, NY[h]	67.7	11.4	0.36	13.6	52.0
Woodbridge, NJ[l]	66.5	10.8	0.38	28.4	102.9
Minneapolis, MN[m]	26.2	6.7	0.24	16.3	60.1
San Francisco, CA[d]	22.5	6.6	0.17	9.5	34.4
Morgantown, WV[n]	119.2	16.8	0.52	26.0	88.5
Moorestown, NJ[l]	62.1	12.4	0.40	25.1	89.5
Jersey City, NJ[l]	14.4	2.2	0.09	8.6	30.8
Casper, WY[d]	9.1	2.8	0.09	5.5	20.4
Freehold, NJ[l]	38.3	16.0	0.44	35.3	130.1

[a] Based on photo-interpretation of tree/shrub cover or satellite-derived cover maps, excluding cities noted with *, which were estimated plot cover data

[b] Pollution removal and values are for carbon monoxide, sulfur and nitrogen dioxide, ozone, and particulate matter less than 10 microns (PM_{10}).

[c] Pollution values updated to 2007 values.

[d] City personnel

[e] ACRT, Inc.

[f] U.S Forest Service and University of California Riverside

[g] Various Departments of the City of Chicago

[h] U.S. Forest Service

[i] Casey Trees Endowment Fund

[j] City personnel, urban boundary of city

[k] Northeast Pennsylvania Urban & Community Forestry Program staff, Keystone College interns, Penn State Extension Urban Forester, and DCNR Bureau of Forestry staff

[l] New Jersey Department of Environmental Protection

[m] Davey Resource Group

[n] West Virginia University

* includes shrub cover in tree cover estimate; based on photo-interpretation or satellite analyses of cover

APPENDIX II. GENERAL RECOMMENDATIONS FOR AIR QUALITY IMPROVEMENT

Urban vegetation can directly and indirectly affect local and regional air quality by altering the urban atmospheric environment. Four main ways that urban trees affect air quality are:

Temperature reduction and other microclimatic effects
Removal of air pollutants
Emission of volatile organic compounds (VOC) and tree maintenance emissions
Energy conservation on buildings and consequent power plant emissions

The cumulative and interactive effects of trees on climate, pollution removal, and VOC and power plant emissions determine the overall impact of trees on air pollution. Cumulative studies involving urban tree impacts on ozone have revealed that increased urban canopy cover, particularly with low VOC emitting species, leads to reduced ozone concentrations in cities. Local urban forest management decisions also can help improve air quality.

Urban forest management strategies to help improve air quality include:

Strategy	Reason
Increase the number of healthy trees	Increase pollution removal
Sustain existing tree cover	Maintain pollution removal levels
Maximize use of low VOC-emitting trees	Reduces ozone and carbon monoxide formation
Sustain large, healthy trees	Large trees have greatest per-tree effects
Use long-lived trees	Reduce long-term pollutant emissions from planting and removal
Use low maintenance trees	Reduce pollutants emissions from maintenance activities
Reduce fossil fuel use in maintaining vegetation	Reduce pollutant emissions
Plant trees in energy conserving locations	Reduce pollutant emissions from power plants
Plant trees to shade parked cars	Reduce vehicular VOC emissions
Supply ample water to vegetation	Enhance pollution removal and temperature reduction
Plant trees in polluted or heavily populated areas	Maximizes tree air quality benefits
Avoid pollutant-sensitive species	Improve tree health
Utilize evergreen trees for particulate matter	Year-round removal of particles

APPENDIX III. RELATIVE TREE EFFECTS

The urban forest in Morgantown provides benefits that include carbon storage and sequestration, and air pollutant removal. To estimate a relative value of these benefits, tree benefits were compared to estimates of average carbon emissions in the city[19], average passenger automobile emissions[20], and average household emissions[21].

General tree information:

Average tree diameter (d.b.h.) = 5.7 in.
Median tree diameter (d.b.h.) = 3.1 in.
Average number of trees per person = 23.0
Number of trees sampled = 1,295
Number of species sampled = 72

Average tree effects by tree diameter:

D.b.h. Class (inch)[a]	Carbon storage			Carbon sequestration			Pollution removal	
	(lbs)	($)	(miles)[a]	(lbs/yr)	($/yr)	(miles)[b]	(lbs/yr)	($/yr)
1-3	7	0.07	30	1.5	0.02	5	0.1	0.23
3-6	52	0.54	190	4.9	0.05	18	0.1	0.56
6-9	170	1.76	620	10.4	0.11	38	0.3	1.12
9-12	376	3.89	1,380	14.2	0.15	52	0.4	1.33
12-15	753	7.79	2,760	23.2	0.24	85	0.5	1.79
15-18	1,200	12.42	4,400	32.1	0.33	117	0.6	2.35
18-21	1,675	17.32	6,130	40.8	0.42	149	1.0	3.93
21-24	2,415	24.98	8,850	44.4	0.46	163	0.8	3.04
24-27	2,898	29.98	10,610	67.5	0.70	247	1.6	6.05
27-30	4,520	46.76	16,550	75.5	0.78	277	1.4	5.31
30+	7,201	74.49	26,370	106.8	1.11	391	1.7	6.27

[a] Lower limit of D.b.h. class is greater than displayed (e.g., 3-6 is actually 3.01 to 6 inches)
[b] miles = number of automobile miles driven that produces emissions equivalent to tree effect

The Morgantown's urban forest provides:

Carbon storage equivalent to:
Amount of carbon (C) emitted in city in 195 days, or
Annual carbon emissions from 56,000 automobiles, or
Annual C emissions from 28,000 single family houses

Annual C sequestration equivalent to:
Amount of C emitted in city in 6.1 days, or
Annual C emissions from 1,700 automobiles, or
Annual C emissions from 900 single family homes

Carbon monoxide removal equivalent to:
Annual carbon monoxide emissions from 6 automobiles, or
Annual carbon monoxide emissions from <1 single family house

Nitrogen dioxide removal equivalent to:
Annual nitrogen dioxide emissions from 400 automobiles, or
Annual nitrogen dioxide emissions from 300 single family houses

Sulfur dioxide removal equivalent to:
Annual sulfur dioxide emissions from 15,400 automobiles, or
Annual sulfur dioxide emissions from 300 single family houses

Particulate matter less than 10 micron (PM_{10}) removal equivalent to:
Annual PM_{10} emissions from 66,200 automobiles, or
Annual PM_{10} emissions from 6,400 single family houses

APPENDIX IV. TREE PLANTING INDEX MAP

To determine the best locations to plant trees, tree canopy and impervious cover maps from National Land Cover Data[22] were used in conjunction with 2000 U.S. Census data to produce a priority planting index (PPI) for areas of Morgantown. Index values were produced for each census block; the higher the index value, the higher the priority of the area for tree planting. This index is a type of "environmental equity" index with areas with higher human population density and lower tree cover tending to get the higher index value. The criteria used to make the index were:

- Population density: the greater the population density, the greater the priority for tree planting
- Tree stocking levels: the lower the tree stocking level (the percent of available greenspace (tree, grass, and soil cover areas) that is occupied by tree canopies), the greater the priority for tree planting
- Tree cover per capita: the lower the amount of tree canopy cover per capita (m²/capita), the greater the priority for tree planting

Each criteria was standardized[23] on a scale of 0 to 1 with 1 representing the census block group with the highest value in relation to priority of tree planting (i.e., the census block group with highest population density, lowest stocking density, or lowest tree cover per capita were standardized to a rating of 1). Individual scores were combined and standardized based on the following formula to produce an overall PPI value between 0 and 100:

$$PPI = (PD * 40) + (TS * 30) + (TPC * 30)$$

Where PPI = index value, PD is standardized population density, TS is standardized tree stocking, and TPC is standardized tree cover per capita. The higher the PPI value, the greater the priority or need for planting trees.

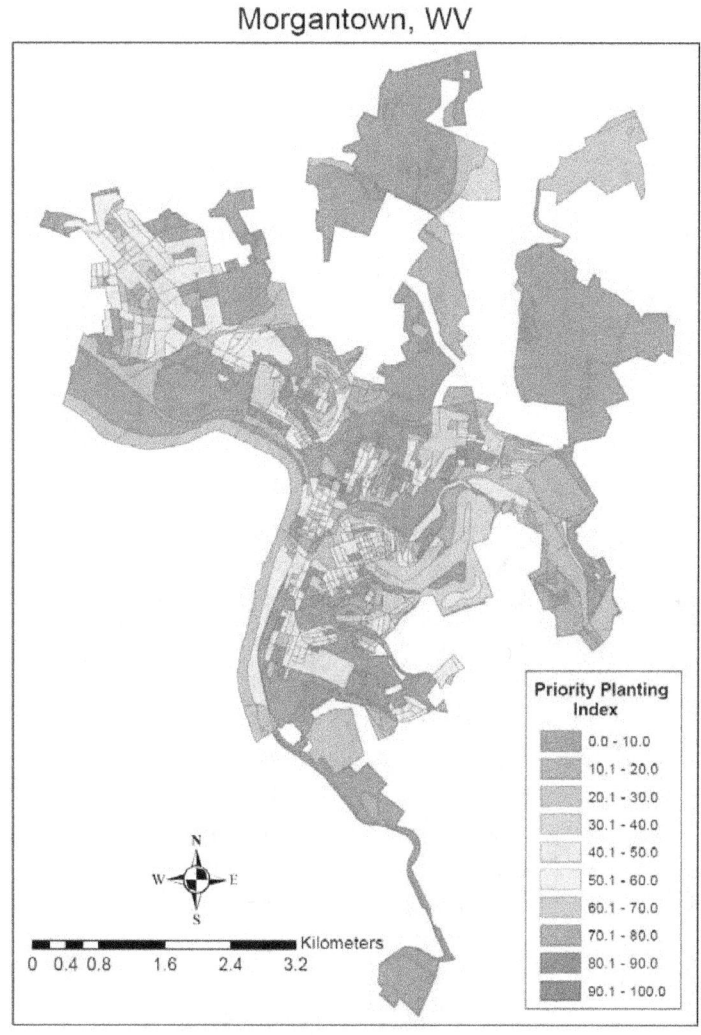

Morgantown, WV

Priority Planting Index

- 0.0 - 10.0
- 10.1 - 20.0
- 20.1 - 30.0
- 30.1 - 40.0
- 40.1 - 50.0
- 50.1 - 60.0
- 60.1 - 70.0
- 70.1 - 80.0
- 80.1 - 90.0
- 90.1 - 100.0

Kilometers
0 0.4 0.8   1.6   2.4   3.2

APPENDIX V. LIST OF SPECIES SAMPLED IN MORGANTOWN

Genus	Species	Common Name	% Population	% Leaf Area	IV[a]
Acer	*campestre*	hedge maple	<0.1	<0.1	0.1
Acer	*negundo*	boxelder	4.5	4.1	8.6
Acer	*nigrum*	black maple	2.7	3.2	5.9
Acer	*palmatum*	Japanese maple	<0.1	<0.1	0.1
Acer	*platanoides*	Norway maple	0.1	0.2	0.3
Acer	*rubrum*	red maple	4.5	6.3	10.8
Acer	*saccharinum*	silver maple	1.5	2.9	4.4
Acer	*saccharum*	sugar maple	14.9	19.1	34.0
Ailanthus	*altissima*	tree-of-heaven	2.9	1.5	4.4
Aralia	*spinosa*	devil's walkingstick	0.1	<0.1	0.1
Carpinus	*caroliniana*	American hornbeam	0.3	0.2	0.5
Carya	*cordiformis*	bitternut hickory	1.4	1.0	2.4
Carya	*glabra*	pignut hickory	0.5	0.6	1.1
Carya	*illinoensis*	pecan	<0.1	<0.1	0.1
Carya	*ovata*	shagbark hickory	0.6	1.5	2.1
Carya	*species*	hickory	<0.1	0.1	0.2
Carya	*tomentosa*	mockernut hickory	<0.1	0.4	0.5
Castanea	*pumila*	Alleghany chinkapin	<0.1	0.8	0.9
Celtis	*occidentalis*	northern hackberry	2.0	1.0	3.0
Cercidiphyllum	*japonicum*	katsura tree	<0.1	0.3	0.4
Cercis	*canadensis*	eastern redbud	0.1	0.1	0.2
Cornus	*florida*	flowering dogwood	1.5	0.7	2.2
Crataegus	*species*	hawthorn	4.8	0.7	5.5
Fagus	*grandifolia*	American beech	1.4	2.1	3.5
Fraxinus	*americana*	white ash	4.1	1.9	6.0
Fraxinus	*pennsylvanica*	green ash	1.9	0.9	2.8
Gleditsia	*triacanthos*	honeylocust	0.1	<0.1	0.1
Ilex	*opaca*	American holly	0.3	0.1	0.4
Juglans	*cinerea*	butternut	<0.1	0.2	0.3
Juglans	*nigra*	black walnut	0.5	1.1	1.6
Juglans	*regia*	English walnut	<0.1	0.2	0.3
Juniperus	*virginiana*	eastern redcedar	<0.1	0.1	0.2
Lindera	*benzoin*	spicebush	2.1	3.5	5.6
Liquidambar	*styraciflua*	sweetgum	<0.1	0.1	0.2
Liriodendron	*tulipifera*	tulip tree	2.2	5.0	7.2
Lonicera	*maackii*	amur honeysuckle	2.6	0.3	2.9
Lonicera	*species*	honeysuckle	0.6	0.1	0.7
Magnolia	*acuminata*	cucumber tree	0.2	0.1	0.3
Magnolia	*species*	magnolia	<0.1	<0.1	0.1
Malus	*species*	crabapple	0.3	0.2	0.5
Morus	*alba*	white mulberry	0.2	0.1	0.3

Continued

Genus	Species	Common Name	% Population	% Leaf Area	IV[a]
Nyssa	*sylvatica*	black tupelo	1.3	0.9	2.2
Picea	*abies*	Norway spruce	1.6	3.1	4.7
Picea	*pungens*	blue spruce	0.6	0.5	1.1
Pinus	*strobus*	eastern white pine	0.1	0.2	0.3
Platanus	*acerifolia*	London planetree	<0.1	0.6	0.7
Platanus	*occidentalis*	American sycamore	0.9	4.4	5.3
Populus	*grandidentata*	bigtooth aspen	<0.1	<0.5	0.1
Prunus	*avium*	sweet cherry	<0.1	0.2	0.3
Prunus	*serotina*	black cherry	7.9	9.0	16.9
Prunus	*species*	cherry	0.4	0.1	0.5
Pyrus	*calleryana*	callery pear	0.2	0.3	0.5
Quercus	*alba*	white oak	0.4	0.4	0.8
Quercus	*palustris*	pin oak	0.3	0.3	0.6
Quercus	*prinus*	chestnut oak	0.2	0.8	1.0
Quercus	*rubra*	northern red oak	1.7	4.3	6.0
Rhododendron	*maximum*	rosebay rhododendron	<0.1	<0.1	0.1
Rhododendron	*species*	rhododendron	<0.1	<0.1	0.1
Rhus	*typhina*	staghorn sumac	<0.1	<0.1	0.1
Robinia	*pseudoacacia*	black locust	4.5	4.0	8.5
Salix	*nigra*	black willow	0.3	0.1	0.4
Sassafras	*albidum*	sassafras	1.1	0.4	1.5
Syringa	*species*	lilac	0.1	0.1	0.2
Thuja	*occidentalis*	northern white-cedar	0.2	0.1	0.3
Tilia	*americana*	American basswood	0.6	0.2	0.8
Tsuga	*canadensis*	eastern hemlock	1.3	1.6	2.9
Ulmus	*americana*	American elm	1.6	1.5	3.1
Ulmus	*rubra*	slippery elm	4.2	5.5	9.7
Viburnum	*prunifolium*	black haw	1.1	0.4	1.5
Viburnum	*rufidulum*	rusty blackhaw	0.5	0.1	0.6
Viburnum	*setigerum*	tea viburnum	0.1	<0.1	0.1
Viburnum	*species*	viburnum	0.5	0.1	0.6
		unknown species -dead	8.3	0.0	8.3

[a] IV = importance value (% population + % leaf area)

REFERENCES

1 Nowak, D.J.; Crane, D.E. 2000. **The Urban Forest Effects (UFORE) Model: quantifying urban forest structure and functions.** In: Hansen, M.; Burk, T., eds. Integrated tools for natural resources inventories in the 21st century. Proceedings of IUFRO conference. Gen. Tech. Rep. NC-212. St. Paul, MN: U.S. Department of Agriculture, Forest Service, North Central Research Station: 714-720.

2 Nowak, D.J.; Crane, D.E.; Stevens, J.C.; Hoehn, R.E. 2005. **The urban forest effects (UFORE) model: field data collection manual.** V1b. [Newtown Square, PA]: U.S. Department of Agriculture, Forest Service, Northeastern Research Station. 34 p. http://www.fs.fed.us/ne/syracuse/Tools/downloads/UFORE_Manual.pdf

3 Nowak, D.J. 1994. **Atmospheric carbon dioxide reduction by Chicago's urban forest.** In: McPherson, E.G.; Nowak, D.J.; Rowntree, R.A., eds. Chicago's urban forest ecosystem: results of the Chicago Urban Forest Climate Project. Gen. Tech. Rep. NE-186. Radnor, PA: U.S. Department of Agriculture, Forest Service, Northeastern Forest Experiment Station: 83-94.

4 Baldocchi, D. 1988. **A multi-layer model for estimating sulfur dioxide deposition to a deciduous oak forest canopy.** Atmospheric Environment. 22: 869-884.

5 Baldocchi, D.D.; Hicks, B.B.; Camara, P. 1987. **A canopy stomatal resistance model for gaseous deposition to vegetated surfaces.** Atmospheric Environment. 21: 91-101.

6 Bidwell, R.G.S.; Fraser, D.E. 1972. **Carbon monoxide uptake and metabolism by leaves.** Canadian Journal of Botany. 50: 1435-1439.

7 Lovett, G.M. 1994. **Atmospheric deposition of nutrients and pollutants in North America: an ecological perspective.** Ecological Applications. 4: 629-650.

8 Zinke, P.J. 1967. **Forest interception studies in the United States.** In: Sopper, W.E.; Lull, H.W., eds. Forest hydrology. Oxford, UK: Pergamon Press: 137-161.

9 McPherson, E.G.; Simpson, J.R. 1999. **Carbon dioxide reduction through urban forestry: guidelines for professional and volunteer tree planters.** Gen. Tech. Rep. PSW-171. Albany, CA: U.S. Department of Agriculture, Forest Service, Pacific Southwest Research Station. 237 p.

10 Nowak, D.J.; Crane, D.E.; Dwyer, J.F. 2002. **Compensatory value of urban trees in the United States.** Journal of Arboriculture. 28(4): 194-199.

11 Nowak, D.J.; Crane, D.E.; Stevens, J.C.; Ibarra, M. 2002. **Brooklyn's urban forest.** Gen. Tech. Rep. NE-290. Newtown Square, PA: U.S. Department of Agriculture, Forest Service, Northeastern Research Station. 107 p.

12 Nowak D.J.; Dwyer, J.F. 2000. **Understanding the benefits and costs of urban forest ecosystems.** In: Kuser, J. E., ed. Handbook of urban and community forestry in the northeast. New York: Kluwer Academics/Plenum: 11-22.

13 Murray, F.J.; Marsh L.; Bradford, P.A. 1994. **New York state energy plan, vol. II: issue reports.** Albany, NY: New York State Energy Office.

These values were updated to 2007 dollars based on the producer price index from U.S Department of Labor, Bureau of Labor Statistics n.d. www.bls.gov/ppi

14 Abdollahi, K.K.; Ning, Z.H.; Appeaning, A., eds. 2000. **Global climate change and the urban forest.** Baton Rouge, LA: GCRCC and Franklin Press. 77 p.

15 Animal and Plant Health Inspection Service. 2010. **Plant Health—Asian longhorned beetle.** Washington, DC: U.S. Department of Agriculture, Animal and Plant Health Inspection Service. http://www.aphis.usda.gov/plant_health/plant_pest_info/asian_lhb/index.shtml

16 Northeastern Area State and Private Forestry. 2005. **Gypsy moth digest.** Newtown Square, PA: U.S. Department of Agriculture, Forest Service, Northeastern Area State and Private Forestry. http://www.na.fs.fed.us/fhp/gm/

17 Michigan State University. 2010. **Emerald ash borer.** East Lansing: MI: Michigan State University [and others]. http://www.emeraldashborer.info

18 Stack, R.W.; McBride, D.K.; Lamey, H.A. 1996. **Dutch elm disease.** PP-324 (revised). Fargo, ND: North Dakota State University, Cooperative Extension Service. http://www.ext.nodak.edu/extpubs/plantsci/trees/pp324w.htm

Explanation of Calculations of Appendix III and IV

19 Total city carbon emissions were based on 2003 U.S. per capita carbon emissions, calculated as total U.S. carbon emissions (Energy Information Administration, 2003, Emissions of Greenhouse Gases in the United States 2003. http://www.eia.doe.gov/oiaf/1605/1605aold.html) divided by 2003 total U.S. population (www.census.gov). Per capita emissions were multiplied by Minneapolis population to estimate total city carbon emissions.

20 Average passenger automobile emissions per mile were based on dividing total 2002 pollutant emissions from light-duty gas vehicles (National Emission Trends http://www.epa.gov/ttn/chief/trends/index.html) by total miles driven in 2002 by passenger cars (National Transportation Statistics http://www.bts.gov/publications/national_transportation_statistics/2004/).

Average annual passenger automobile emissions per vehicle were based on dividing total 2002 pollutant emissions from light-duty gas vehicles by total number of passenger cars in 2002 (National Transportation Statistics http://www.bts.gov/publications/national_transportation_statistics/2004/).

Carbon dioxide emissions from automobiles assumed 6 pounds of carbon per gallon of gasoline with energy costs of refinement and transportation included (Graham, R.L.; Wright, L.L.; Turhollow, A.F. 1992. The potential for short-rotation woody crops to reduce U.S. CO_2 emissions. Climatic Change. 22: 223-238.)

21 Average household emissions based on average electricity kWh usage, natural gas Btu usage, fuel oil Btu usage, kerosene Btu usage, LPG Btu usage, and wood Btu usage per household from:

Energy Information Administration. Total Energy Consumption in U.S. Households by Type of Housing Unit, 2001 www.eia.doe.gov/emeu/recs/recs2001/detailcetbls.html.

CO_2, SO_2, and NO_x power plant emission per KWh from:

U.S. Environmental Protection Agency. U.S. power plant emissions total by year www.epa.gov/cleanenergy/egrid/samples.htm.

CO emission per kWh assumes one-third of 1 percent of C emissions is CO based on:

Energy Information Administration. 1994. Energy use and carbon emissions: non-OECD countries. DOE/EIA-0579(94). Washington, DC: Department of Energy, Energy Information Administration. http://tonto.eia.doe.gov/bookshelf

PM10 emission per kWh from:

Layton, M. 2004. 2005 Electricity environmental performance report: electricity generation and air emissions. Sacramento, CA: California Energy Commission. http://www.energy.ca.gov/2005_energypolicy/documents/2004-11-15_workshop/2004-11-15_03- A_LAYTON.PDF

CO_2, NO_x, SO_2, PM_{10}, and CO emission per Btu for natural gas, propane and butane (average used to represent LPG), Fuel #4 and #6 (average used to represent fuel oil and kerosene) from:

Abraxas energy consulting. http://www.abraxasenergy.com/emissions/

CO_2 and fine particle emissions per Btu of wood from:

Houck, J.E.; Tiegs, P.E.; McCrillis, R.C.; Keithley, C.; Crouch, J. 1998. Air emissions from residential heating: the wood heating option put into environmental perspective. In: Proceedings of U.S. EPA and Air and Waste Management Association conference: living in a global environment, V.1: 373-384

CO, NO_x and SO_x emission per Btu of wood based on total emissions from wood burning (tonnes) from:

Residential Wood Burning Emissions in British Columbia. 2005. http://www.env.gov.bc.ca/air/airquality/pdfs/wood_emissions.pdf.

Emissions per dry tonne of wood converted to emissions per Btu based on average dry weight per cord of wood and average Btu per cord from:

Kuhns, M.; Schmidt, T. 1988. Heating with wood: species characteristics and volumes I. NebGuide G-88-881-A. Lincoln, NE: University of Nebraska, Institute of Agriculture and Natural Resources, Cooperative Extension.

22 National Land Cover Data available at: www.epa.gov/mrlc/nlcd.html.

23 Standardized value for population density was calculated as: $PD = (n - m) / r$
where:
PD is the value (0-1)
n is the value for the census block (population / km^2)
m is the minimum value for all census blocks, and
r is the range of values among all census blocks (maximum value – minimum value).

Standardized value for tree stocking was calculated as: $TS = (1 - (T/(T+G)))$
where:
TS is the value (0-1)
T is percent tree cover, and
G is percent grass cover.

Standardized value for tree cover per capita was calculated as: $TPC = 1 - [(n - m) / r]$
where:
TPC is the value (0-1)
n is the value for the census block (m^2/capita)
m is the minimum value for all census blocks, and
r is the range of values among all census blocks (maximum value – minimum value).

Photo by Anne Cumming, U.S. Forest Service